Resi**** *

T

MW00935728

Cover design by Kirk DouPonce, DogEared Design

Jeremy

Be blessed my friend

Clark 2   Janice K Lee

RESISTING

THE BATTLE AGAINST INERTIA

SUCCESS

CHARMAS B. LEE and **JANICE K. LEE**

Foreword by **RICHARD FAGERLIN**, Author of *Trustology*

TESTIMONIALS

I found *Resisting Success* by Charmas Lee to be a book that had me contemplating my daily choices. From Chapter 1 I was asking myself, 'do I do that?' The honest answer to myself was 'yes'. I can totally relate to the challenges and struggles that Charmas presents and I love the suggestions he offers to help find a resolution. As a 54-year old school teacher, mother, and wife my life is busy and it is easy to use the 'tired' excuse whenever convenient. I enjoyed reading the stories about why and how to not give into the temptation of the excuse. This book is a great read from page one but it is also a book to keep on the shelf as a resource for times when the struggle starts to overwhelm you. Rereading the stories and the exercises is a way to get back on track and realign with the goals you have set and the direction you want to follow. If you are a person who strives to lead a successful life then this book is a great tool to have in your toolbox. I felt a renewed sense of direction and commitment as a result of reading Resisting Success. Thank you Charmas for sharing your life lessons and the insight you have found because of them.

Maureen Brown
Math Teacher
Mitchell High School

What I appreciate and admire most about the book *Resisting Success, The Battle Against Inertia* is the way in which the book maintains a positive, encouraging, safe haven for the reader while at the same time challenging and inspiring the reader to be his/her best! The book references situations and stories and presents exercises and learning opportunities that encompass all aspects of a person: mind, body, and spirit. While reading this book, I had so many "aha" moments that I lost count, and I found myself contemplating many of the topics presented in the book even hours after finishing each chapter.

Sarah King,
Counselor, Class of 2019
Pine Creek High School

Whether we are aware of it or not, we all have behaviors and habits that derail us from achieving all that is possible. As a college student, I find myself letting procrastination and technology get in my way. Charmas Lee not only exposes those behaviors but also provides tools to move beyond them. If you'd like to move beyond those behaviors *Resisting Success* is the book for you.

Mackenzie Howie
University of Northern Colorado Student

Resisting Success is a fun loving self-check book about how we let outside forces (Inertia) get in the way of reaching our full potential. The enclosed exercises will help you overcome those internal and external forces. Be prepared to go on a journey of self-discovery! As business owners, inertia is a daily struggle as we unlock the doors of the office. We must resist inertia to become successful with the growing demands of the healthcare world.

Dr. Dale "Chris" Buckhaults, DC and Ginger Buckhaults
DC Family Chiropractic, Inc

Charmas Lee's "Resisting Success" is stacked with coaching brilliance and snippets that you'll want to use in motivational posters for your wall and on your social media! Coach Lee's character and leadership insights will help anyone win at life. I recommend this book for middle schoolers and those in their golden years alike. His words will not only sharpen how you see yourself, but will give you a good shot of inspiration to keep your relationships healthy. If you truly want to grow your personality and learn to "embrace success," read this book with a pen in hand and take notes as you yield to Coach Lee's wisdom. Then go out, run your race, and finish strong!

Kristan Gray
Author, *No One Could Know*

Our son, Walker loves football, but after a couple of serious injuries in middle school, we were looking for a new sport in high school. Walker had tried track as a 4th grader and enjoyed it so we thought we would give track and field another look. He was completing his 8th grade year when Walker found the triple jump. He was hooked.

We were referred to Speed Track and Field by a mutual friend and thought we would give it a try. We joined the summer before Walker's freshman year and he showed great promise and had a great first season. The love and commitment that Coach Lee and his staff show to his athletes is like no other. They truly love them all and they treat each athlete like they are part of the Lee family. We felt that way from the beginning. I love that Coach Lee referred to Dr. Phil McGraw in this book. Coach Lee is like Dr. Phil in that he will tell you the truth- black and white, straight up truth. It may not be what you want to hear, but it is usually what you need to hear. This is a wonderful trait in a coach: no sugar coating, but love and the truth.

Coach Lee's practices are well thought out, planned and specific to the task. The athletes work hard for him and for themselves. They want to and they do succeed. It is a challenging environment because Coach Lee demands

100%, but there is love, acceptance, and a sense of family like I have never seen. You truly become part of the family at Speed Track and Field. Coach Lee says in the book, "our value is determined by the number of lives we touch in a positive way." Coach Lee has given Walker value in victory & defeat. Coach Lee is not just a track and field coach, he is a life coach.

By reading any of Coach Lee's books, you will feel love, encouragement, and the ability to wake your own inner athlete....to get it done! Don't let inertia take you down. You can't always be right, but you can choose to always be happy and happiness brings great success. Because of Coach Lee, Mrs. Lee and Coach Moon, we will always be a part of the Speed Track and Field family and work to be the best we can in all that we do. You will not be disappointed in any of his books, talks or agendas. Coach Lee is one of a kind! Enjoy all he has to offer.

Jody Council
Mom

Great advice about how to transform your behavior to create joy and success in your life.

Wyatt Weiland
Pine Creek High School Senior

Foreword

Acknowledgements

Introduction

FOREWORD

If you are interested in real results with real impact and real success this book is for you. Resisting success challenges readers to look at the internal battles facing them and to hit them face on in order to overcome the inertia keeping them from achieving breakthrough results. Charmas Lee has been a coach and leader for over 30 years and has dedicated his life to helping people achieve their highest level of greatness. With short and practical chapters this book provides tools and a solid look in the mirror to help you get unstuck and be the best version of you possible.

Richard Fagerlin
Founder and President, Peak Solutions
Author, *Trustology, The Art and Science of High Trust Teams*

ACKNOWLEDGEMENTS

Writing *Resisting Success* was the collaborative effort of many. I'd like to express my thanks to my friend and brother in Christ, Richard Fagerlin for taking time from his busy schedule to read *Resisting Success* and find it worthy to write the foreword. I'd also like to thank my niece Christina Timp. Christina thank you for sharing all of those great books with me which in turn inspired me to write *Resisting Success*. I also express my gratitude to Maureen, Sarah, Mackenzie, Chris, Ginger, Kristan, Jody and Wyatt for taking the time to write the reviews/testimonials. Last but certainly not least I thank my wife Janice for co-authoring this book with me. Thank you for joining me on this endeavor. You are a precious gift from above and I thank God for you each and every day.

INTRODUCTION

Resisting Success is a transparent look at the behaviors, thoughts and fixed action patterns that derail us from achieving our desired outcomes in life. The name that I have assigned to these saboteurs is **inertia**. Inertia takes on many forms. For the runner, it is the invisible force that acts as resistance at the start of the race when the block exit is performed. For the student, inertia may take on the form of procrastination which many consider to be the primary enemy of success. For others inertia raises its ugly head in the form of fear, apprehension, or self-doubt. **Inertia** may manifest itself in our attitudes, prejudices, and bias. For the dreamer, inertia may take on the form of complacency and the cost of inaction is rewarded by the bitter taste of disappointment. One of **inertia's** greatest weapons lives in our internal narrative. It may be the voice of reason that propels us forward or the chorus of despair that leads us to surrender to the pain when victory is right around the corner.

In these chapters, you will discover not only what **your inertia** is, but how to recognize it and conquer it in your own life. My hope is that you will begin to recognize and rectify those behaviors **(inertia)** that may be robbing you of your joy and success and commit to making a permanent transformation. At the end of each chapter you will find exercises and practical tips that will assist you with defeating **inertia**!

Resisting Success
The Battle Against Inertia

Chapter One

The Story I'll Tell Myself

Resisting Success
The Battle Against Inertia

As a coach of 29 years, I have become a BIG fan of Dr. Phillip McGraw. I appreciate his no-nonsense approach to effecting change. I read his book *"Life Strategies"* back in the late 90's and I still apply many of the principles that I learned back then today.

Chapter One is titled **Get Real**. It is about becoming completely honest with yourself and acknowledging the behaviors that are of no value to you. In the book, there is a homework assignment titled **Reality Check** where he asks the reader to sit down and write a story. The story is titled "The story I will tell myself" if I don't create meaningful and lasting change after reading and studying this book.

Well, I wrote the story and finished the book. I identified several behaviors that were moving me in the opposite direction of where I wanted to go. I determined the single most important behavior that if changed would bring tremendous benefit to my life. My goal was to focus on this single behavior for twenty-one days. For the first week, I was consistent and making great progress,

Resisting Success
The Battle Against Inertia

however about ten days in, **inertia**, reared its ugly head. I lost momentum and before I knew it, the twenty-one days had elapsed.

On the twenty-second day, I received a letter in the mail. I had shared the story with a friend of mine, given him an envelope and asked him to mail the envelope to me at the end of the twenty-one days.

When I opened the letter, I became frustrated and immediately began to use my typical excuses, rationalizations, and justifications for my failure. This was a **GREAT** wake up call. There was no one to blame but myself and it was time to get real. I had come face to face with the enemy and the enemy was me. I had to stop letting myself off the hook and tell it like it is. I could choose to be right (in my own mind) instead of happy. I tried the exercise again and the second time around I did much better. The changed behavior transformed my life.

Resisting Success

The Battle Against Inertia

Lesson Learned:

In order to change a behavior, you must first change the **attitude** towards the behavior. A change in behavior must be wrestled with, talked through and come to terms with. As time passed, and by the grace of God, the new behavior became routine. By conquering **inertia,** I developed the proper framework for decision making and have given myself the ability to choose my destination in life.

Resisting Success

The Battle Against Inertia

Chapter One Exercise

The Story I Will Tell Myself

Determine the single most important thing you believe you'd like to accomplish in the next 21 days and make a commitment to concentrate on achieving it.

_____

_____

Determine the type of resources required e.g., accountability partner, financial resources etc.

_____

_____

Determine the process you will use to accomplish this goal e.g., short term goals with benchmarks.

_____

_____

Establish a time line e.g.,

Start Date_____ Finish Date_____

Resisting Success
The Battle Against Inertia

In the event that you fall short of reaching your goal, write down your excuses and justifications for failing. Hand this to your accountability partner and have him/her mail it to you in twenty-one days. Title the page "The Story I Will Tell Myself".

_____

_____

_____

_____

_____

_____

_____

_____

_____

_____

_____

_____

_____

Chapter Two

Integrity

Resisting Success
The Battle Against Inertia

One morning I met my friend Jeff for coffee. Jeff is someone who I deeply admire and hold in high esteem. He is the most intelligent man I have ever met. He doesn't like for me to say it, however at the age of 56 I have met thousands and thousands of people and there is no one like him. His intellect is not the only admirable trait that he possesses. My friend operates from the strength of his highest self. He refuses to simply settle for a lesser version of who he has been created to be. He is a leader by example, genuine, authentic and has a sincere appreciation for his fellow man.

When Jeff arrived, I handed him a cup that holds thirty ounces of water followed by a drink that Jeff calls the "Charmas Special." The "Charmas Special" is three shots of espresso, caramel drizzle and whip cream. This drink is not for the meek at heart!

Jeff and I began our conversation like we typically do, catching up on what's been going on in each other's lives. Jeff shared with me that he had been in Florida for several days. The trip was both business and pleasure. At the end of the trip, he boarded a plane destined to arrive at Denver International Airport (DIA) and then he drove approximately seventy miles or so to Monument, Colorado where he lives. Jeff's next order of business was to drive his son to California where he would intern with a major company. Once this mission was accomplished he caught a plane to Baltimore for a four-day business trip. Jeff then boarded a plane in Baltimore and flew back to DIA and made the seventy-mile drive back to Monument.

Friday morning Jeff took care of some things around his home and arrived promptly at 8:45 AM for our 9:00 meeting. Jeff and I are on what we call Lombardi time. Our motto being, *"if you are 10 minutes early you are 5 minutes late."* As Jeff was sharing this information with me he never complained. Jeff understands the power of full engagement. He knows how to make each day a glorified exhibition of brilliance.

Resisting Success
The Battle Against Inertia

Jeff chugged down thirty ounces of water and slammed back the "Charmas Special". With a smile, he asked me how things had been going for me. My wife and I own two businesses that specialize in performance and achievement, one of which has recently transitioned into the academic arena. I shared with Jeff that our last two weeks had been equally demanding, a whirlwind of meetings, speaking engagements, bidding on contracts, etc. Our travel had been limited to the state of Colorado, however our days had been very long. We are entrepreneurs and on average we work about fourteen hours a day, typically six to seven days a week. "Isn't it great to be an entrepreneur?" I asked Jeff, he said "You bet, there's nothing like freedom coupled with uncertainty ☺"

Now some of you may ask what did I mean by making each day a glorified exhibition of brilliance? For Jeff and me it is simple. Each day we have an opportunity to serve others. Each morning we celebrate one more day. As an entrepreneur, our journey is not easy and uncertainty is guaranteed. We have learned

Resisting Success
The Battle Against Inertia

to celebrate life for its own sake. We are servant leaders. I would say that service before self is the underlying theme of our existence. We understand that our lifetime value will not be determined by the size of our 401(k), our zip code or the kind of vehicle we drive. When the dust clears and it is all said and done our value will be determined by the number of lives we have impacted in a positive way.

I'm sure that when Jeff woke up that morning he was exhausted, operating in a fatigued state. After all, he had been on the road for several days, involved in meetings and had family responsibilities as well. It would have been easy for Jeff to cancel our appointment that morning. **Inertia** in the form of fatigue, was knocking on Jeff's door reminding him how tired he was, and perhaps it made more sense to cancel the meeting with me than to attend it. "*After all, Charmas is your friend*" **inertia** *whispered in his ear, "He will understand. Cancel the meeting, get some rest, go back to bed, you deserve it!"*

Resisting Success

The Battle Against Inertia

Inertia was relentless and kept knocking, but Jeff did not open the door. It would have been easy to resist success by cancelling the appointment, instead my friend Jeff overcame **inertia** and embraced success.

Lesson Learned:

Inertia hates commitment. We build trust when we keep our word and our commitments. With trust our relationships flourish, productivity rises and we have a high degree of personal and professional satisfaction. Trust is the one thing that determines the success of our teams and our business and personal relationships.

Resisting Success
The Battle Against Inertia

Chapter Two Exercise

Personal Score Card

In the blanks below identify five areas to work on (e.g., timeliness, attentiveness, trustworthiness, etc.) to improve your integrity and score them daily.

0-Poor 1-Fair 2-Good 3-Average 4-Above Average 5-Excellent

1. _____ 0   1   2   3   4   5

2. _____ 0   1   2   3   4   5

3. _____ 0   1   2   3   4   5

4. _____ 0   1   2   3   4   5

5. _____ 0   1   2   3   4   5

Resisting Success
The Battle Against Inertia

Chapter Three

Fear

Faith

Focus

Follow Through

Resisting Success
The Battle Against Inertia

For several years I've had the honor of being mentored (coached) both personally and professionally by a gentleman named Tim Devore. Tim is my kind of coach. He is brilliant, a man of God, has a stunning intellect and possesses a powerful business acumen. Tim is the President of DeVore, Inc. and has worked with hundreds of CEOs, Presidents, and C level staff to improve their productivity. While in the Air Force Tim was a combat navigator; now he successfully helps others navigate their personal and professional lives. Tim has a heart of gold, however, when it comes to getting things accomplished he is a no-nonsense kind of guy. He doesn't accept excuses of any kind.

I sought Tim out for some business advice. In our first coaching session, Tim asked me questions that I had never thought about and was certainly not prepared to answer. He asked me about my net-worth and my life plan. Tim said that to develop a blue print for success it would be important to know these things. By the end of the phone call I had a list of questions that I was not

Resisting Success
The Battle Against Inertia

sure how to answer. We scheduled a follow-up call in fourteen days. Feeling overwhelmed, I hung up the phone and walked upstairs scratching my head. I began to second-guess my decision to ask for Tim's assistance, **inertia** kicked in.

My wife Janice looked at me and said, "What's wrong sweetheart, are you feeling OK?" "Sweetheart" I replied, "I wasn't equipped to answer any of Tim's questions, it's like I brought a knife to a gun fight!" Without skipping a beat Janice said "Well what are you going to do? Now you know what it feels like to be one of your athletes when you ask them the question, do you want to be a champion? Of course, they do, but are they willing to do what is required of them?"

My wife is very good at offering clarity and inspiration. She has a uniqueness about her. She puts things in a context that makes sense to me. Janice will tell you that she speaks "Charmas".

I answered Tim's questions in detail and sent them to him two days later. I guess I passed the "Tim-test"! Over the last few years Tim has tasked me with many things to do. He asks the tough questions, the ones that can take you way out of your comfort zone. Once, in a single conversation Tim asked me the same question three times. He really wanted me to think through my response. "Charmas that is not what I asked you" he'd say, "Please answer the question." So, he would ask me again and again. When I finally answered the question, he'd say thank you, now you can make an informed decision and take decisive action. Tim wanted me to be successful.

Just a few months ago one of our businesses was treading water. Most of my efforts to recruit new business were not working so I reached out to Tim. His advice was to change my focus, change my approach and change my goal.

"Charmas, I want you to find a CEO whose organization is valued at a minimum of $10,000,000. Walk in their office and hand them your media kit." I was dumbfounded. I didn't know anyone in those types of circles. The chorus of despair (**Inertia**) began to sing

Resisting Success
The Battle Against Inertia

aloud in my head asking "fear focused" questions. Do you have time for this? YOU aren't good enough to meet with one of those guys! Why doesn't Tim introduce you to one of his colleagues instead? This is going to take a lot of work, it's probably impossible! You won't make it past the receptionist, blah, blah, blah. After a few moments, I realized that the way I viewed this **opportunity** was the problem. I was fear focused rather than faith focused.

I love the way that Theodore Roosevelt describes and offers a clarifying statement in his inaugural address on March 4, 1933. He suggests that fear is "nameless, unreasoning, unjustified terror which paralyzes needed efforts to convert retreat into advance."

On this occasion, I defeated **inertia** and met with a CEO whose organization was valued at $1,000,000,000. The meeting was scheduled to last 15 minutes, instead it lasted for 45 minutes. It turned out that the CEO and I were more alike than I ever could have imagined and had similar philosophies about life, community and faith. As I drove away from that meeting I asked myself this question; *"How much is fear paying me to give up on my dreams?"*

Lesson Learned:

Coach Tim has carried me to heights I never could have achieved on my own. That is the mark of a true coach. One of the paradoxes in life is that the fear of failure makes failure more likely. Fear makes you play it safe. It makes you play small. Every time I choose fear, apprehension or self-doubt, **inertia** wins and I resist success. To defeat **inertia** it will require faithfulness, reliability, and persistent consistence. Inertia hates faithfulness and commitment.

Resisting Success

The Battle Against Inertia

Chapter Three Exercise

What could we accomplish if we were not afraid?

1. _____
2. _____
3. _____

How does fear show up in my life?

1. _____
2. _____
3. _____

Identify my 3 biggest fears.

1. _____
2. _____
3. _____

Formula to overcome fear:

Recognize-Release-Reprogram

Three affirmations to counter my fears:

1. _____
2. _____
3. _____

Resisting Success

The Battle Against Inertia

Chapter Four

Habits

"I wear the chain I forged in life, I made it link by link, and yard by yard; I girded it on of my own free will, and of my own free will I wore it." — Charles Dickens, A Christmas Carol

"Habits are the chains we forge in life." — Charmas B. Lee

Resisting Success

The Battle Against Inertia

Brendon Burchard is one of the world's greatest high performance coaches. He is world renowned for improving human productivity. His client list includes several Fortune 500 companies and celebrities such as Oprah Winfrey. I have read his books and a few years ago took his Achievement Accelerator online course. Both have made a significant impact in my personal and professional life. Mr. Burchard suggests that it is imperative that we "make common sense common practice." It sounds like a simple thing to do; however, I must confess that this is an area of my life that could use some improvement.

For example, as a coach I recognize the direct correlation between discipline and success. There is no doubt that the disciplined athlete will reach higher heights than the non-disciplined athlete. Practices should be deliberate, highly structured, and highly organized to position the athlete for the best chance of success. Well, common sense would suggest that if there are areas

Resisting Success
The Battle Against Inertia

in my life that I'd like to be more productive in, then perhaps those areas should be more deliberate, organized and structured.

There is one part of my day that I know if I follow protocol will yield a tremendous benefit to myself and others. It is the morning. I've learned to be territorial with my mornings. When I do, my days run smoother, I have more energy and I can bring the energy, attitude, and joy to just about every situation. However, when I chose **inertia**, rather than common sense, it becomes very apparent that I have **resisted success**. In fact, on those mornings that I don't make common sense common practice I can **guarantee** my success as a failure!

Here is what my successful morning looks like. Upon awakening I pause and befriend silence. I've learned that it is important for me to listen to my thoughts. The term which best describes this behavior is metacognition which, in laymen's terms, means thinking about thinking. Neuroscience suggests that the brain processes 45-60k thoughts daily and up to 85% of those

Resisting Success
The Battle Against Inertia

thoughts are repetitive. The truth be told, at any moment of the day we are either selling ourselves on ourselves or selling ourselves out.

According to Napoleon Bonaparte, "there are 15 minutes in every battle that will determine the outcome of the war." My 15 minutes occurs in the morning. Research indicates that the first three thoughts we have in the morning can direct our path for the day, therefore I pay close attention to my self-talk or internal narrative. I have developed a system I call **Think-Say-Do** to make sure that I embrace the proper psychological and emotional attitude for the day. The exercise only takes about 15 seconds.

Upon awakening I close my eyes, turn my attention inward, silence my mind and listen to my thoughts. This is called metacognition. If my morning thoughts do not align themselves with my purpose in life, I change them, however I have learned that *sometimes you have to storm before you norm.* In other words, achieving success in this area will require consistent persistence.

Resisting Success
The Battle Against Inertia

Step 1. As I **Think** I Become

My first 3 thoughts (internal) are "Powerful, Impactful, Purposeful". These words align themselves with my mission in life.

Step 2. As I **See** I Believe

It is not enough to simply think these three words it is important to see the words either in a printed form or through your mind's eye.

Step 3. As I **Say** (speak) I create

My first 3 words communicated outwardly are "Powerful, Impactful, Purposeful". Thoughts and words are neutral. We assign the value to them.

Step 4. As I **Seize** I take hold of.

By adding the prefix, "I am", to my words I operate in the present and then, I boldly **say** what I **see** and **seize** what I say.
I am Powerful-I am Impactful-I am Purposeful

Step 5. I **Do** with intention, passion and enthusiasm.

This empowers me to choose the attitude I will embrace for the day.

The next step is to express my gratitude. I do this by leaning over and kissing my beautiful wife on the forehead. We

Resisting Success
The Battle Against Inertia

have a small breed mastiff who sleeps with us and his name is Epic. I realize that a small breed mastiff is an oxymoron nonetheless I pat him on the head, letting him know he is appreciated also.

My next order of business is to roll to my left and get out of bed. Once my feet hit the floor I express my gratitude again, thanking God for one more day. Turning to my night stand I reach for my water and consume 30 ounces. I live in Colorado Springs, Colorado at an elevation of approximately 6000 feet. I know that if you dehydrate the body by three percent it slows down the contractile speed of the muscle by eight percent and muscle power by ten percent (by the way the brain is a muscle too). Dehydration can lead to a lack of concentration and focus. It will increase the heart's workload by ten percent which will affect clarity and performance.

Next, I head downstairs to my human performance lab and train cardio and strength for thirty to forty-five minutes. During this time, I listen to spiritual music. This allows me to spend time with

Resisting Success
The Battle Against Inertia

God and helps me get pumped up for the day. Upon completion of my workout I caffeinate, fuel, shower, get dressed and chose the attitude that I will embrace for the day.

An abbreviated version of the complete ritual looks like this.

1. Think - 3 thoughts or words
2. See - 3 thoughts or words in my mind's eye
3. Say - 3 thoughts or words
4. Seize - 3 thoughts or words by adding I am
5. Do with intention, passion and enthusiasm
6. Express Gratitude i.e. wife, dog, feet touch the ground
7. Drink 24-30 ounces of water
8. Affirmation (Set my intention for the day)
9. Don't check my inbox, texts (checks me out of my life)
10. Physical Training-Spiritual Training-Mental Training
11. Fuel
12. Embrace the attitude I will chose for the day!

Resisting Success

The Battle Against Inertia

Over the years I have collected valid, reliable data and am certain that by following this protocol I am choosing success. Every time I chose success I cripple **inertia** and render its efforts to derail me useless for the day. Sometimes **inertia** will use technology to distract me so I do not turn on my computer or check any text messages or emails before completing my AM ritual.

Lesson Learned:

Obedience is better than sacrifice. Performing this simple act of obedience (my AM ritual) increases my productivity by five to ten percent, allowing me to move through each day with grace and ease. I recognize that once I flip the switch on technology I am on someone else's agenda.

Resisting Success

The Battle Against Inertia

Chapter Four Exercise

AM Flight Checklist

Date: _____

As I think I become.

My first 3-thoughts or words *(internal)* upon awakening

- ✓ _____
- ✓ _____
- ✓ _____

As I speak I create.

My first 3-things that I communicate(*external*) outwardly?

- ✓ _____
- ✓ _____
- ✓ _____

I do with …

- ✓ _____
- ✓ _____
- ✓ _____

Resisting Success

The Battle Against Inertia

AM Ritual

1._____

2._____

3._____

4._____

5._____

6._____

Chapter Five

Procrastination - The Cost of Inaction

Resisting Success
The Battle Against Inertia

According to the late Stephen Covey, "Anything less than a conscious commitment to the important is an unconscious commitment to the unimportant." In other words, keep the priority the priority! We all know that procrastination is the enemy of success. I encourage my clients to get rid of anything that is not moving the needle toward their growth, contribution, joy or impact. Unfortunately, I have been bitten by the procrastination bug many times. Inaction carries with it a hefty price tag.

Most people do not become aware of the present until it becomes the past. Timing is everything. On February 14, 1876, Alexander Graham Bell filed an application for a patent for his version of the telephone. On that very same day a gentleman named Elisha Gray (whom most have never heard of) applied for a *caveat* announcing his **intention** to file a claim for a patent for the same invention within three months. Based on Bell's earlier filing time, a mere few hours, the U.S. Patent Office awarded Bell, not Gray, the patent for the telephone.

Resisting Success
The Battle Against Inertia

Elisha Gray passed away in 1901. Discovered among his belongings was a note addressing his lingering disappointment concerning the telephone. This is a very simple example of the cost of inaction. Most of us don't know the name Elisha Gray, while Bell is a household name.

I am not sure if Elisha gray was a procrastinator or not but when I read the story it prompted me to took a deeper look at my own behaviors and in doing so I observed three different types of procrastination.

1. **The Functional Procrastinator:**

   The functional procrastinator's behavior isn't always negative. It represents an **acceptable, frequent** behavior which increases success and acts as a success strategy towards a pre-designed goal that generally results in success.

Resisting Success

2. **The Productive Procrastinator:**

   The productive procrastinator's perspective is "why do today what you can do the day after tomorrow?"

3. **The Master Procrastinator:**

   The master procrastinator encourages fun tasks over productive, sensible ones or prefers to do the less important tasks only to find themselves in a crisis management mode.

I am not sure if you fall into one or more of these categories, but some years ago I would have been labeled a master procrastinator. I came face to face with the enemy and the enemy was me. My definition of procrastination was putting things off to the last minute. There are several theories on why this phenomenon occurs, but let's leave that for a later time. Like many others I battled this wretched foe for years and time after time I fell prey to its power. My cost of inaction was very high, resulting in

Resisting Success

The Battle Against Inertia

loss of income, increased stress and anxiety, feelings of poor self-worth, etc.

There are hundreds of books on the topic. While doing some research I came across a book titled *The Power of Focus*. There was a total chapter dedicated to the topic and it turned out to be very helpful. One of the things that I gleamed from the book was in order to change a behavior, you must change your attitude towards the behavior. That is when the light came on for me and I began to conquer **inertia.**

Resisting Success

The Battle Against Inertia

Lesson Learned:

There was a hidden cost associated with procrastination that I had never considered. It was how I treated the people that I love. I kept a journal for two weeks and it was easy to see that when I procrastinated, I didn't show up within the strength of my highest self. I didn't treat those I love like royalty. I displaced blame and did not accept responsibility for the outcomes. Well, that was then and this I now. Inertia has lost its grip and I get things done timely and in order.

Resisting Success

The Battle Against Inertia

Chapter Five Exercise

Behavior Modification Framework

A. Behavior _____

B. Negative Consequences *(Build a case for change)*

_____

C. What is my pay off *(what's in it for me?)*

_____

D. Triggers actions observed prior to behavior

_____

E. Action Step Become aware of triggers.

_____

F. By taking this action what are the positive outcomes?

_____

G. Successful New Behavior

_____

Step-wise approach

1. _____
2. _____
3. _____

Resisting Success

The Battle Against Inertia

Chapter Six

Excuse Me?

Resisting Success

The Battle Against Inertia

As a young boy growing up in Colorado Springs, Colorado, my parents gave me chores to do. Sometimes my friends would be out playing basketball at the park or swimming, but I couldn't leave the house until I finished my chores. Often, I'd strike up a conversation with my mom and ask information seeking questions. For example, "Mom, why do I have to take out the trash and my friends Arthur and John are playing at the park?" Mom would say "Because I said so!"

It is funny how time repeats itself. My children have asked that same information seeking question. While my response is a little different than my mom's it is equally effective. In those moments I am often reminded of the story of *A Message to Garcia*.

A *Message to Garcia* is the story of 24-year-old West Point graduate Army 1LT Andrew Rowan. When war broke out between Spain and the United States, it was necessary to communicate quickly with Calixto Garcia, one of the three top commanders of the Cuban rebels and leader of the insurgence. Recognizing this was

Resisting Success
The Battle Against Inertia

a pivotal time in the war President McKinley needed to get a message to Garcia. They believed Garcia was somewhere in Cuba, however no one knew exactly where he was.

Someone said to the President, "There's a fellow by the name of Rowan who will find Garcia for you, if anybody can." Rowan was sent for and told directly to "Get this message to Garcia!" Rowan wasn't offered any other instructions or details about the journey…nor did he ask! Rowan took the letter, sealed it up in an oil-skin pouch and strapped it over his heart. Four days later he landed by night off the coast of Cuba from an open boat and disappeared into the jungle.

Three weeks later he came out on the other side of the hostile country and had accomplished the task of getting the message to Garcia. The point being, Rowan delivered the message with no questions asked. He didn't complain or attempt to displace the responsibility. 1Lt Rowan embraced success by resisting **inertia**.

Resisting Success

The Battle Against Inertia

Lesson Learned:

It is important to honor the requests of those in authority. Sometimes not having the details can take us on an adventure of a lifetime. It encourages us to use our imagination.

Resisting Success
The Battle Against Inertia

Chapter Six Exercise

What would my life be like if there were no excuses?

Take a moment to define the difference between an excuse and a reason.

Excuse:

_____

_____

_____

Reason:

_____

_____

_____

What are your top five excuses?

1. _____
2. _____
3. _____
4. _____
5. _____

Resisting Success

The Battle Against Inertia

Chapter Seven

Tied to Technology…A Humorous Anecdote 😊

Resisting Success
The Battle Against Inertia

Thanks to technology many of our daily tasks only require a fraction of the time they did just a few years ago. It is easy to fool yourself into believing that with technology we have simplified our lives. Here is what I mean.

Today I answered my phone by using my watch. Reading what I just wrote cracks me up... *I look at my watch to answer my phone, how crazy is that?*

I guess in and of itself, this isn't a big deal but I should have been resting. My intention was to take a nap, however the sound of the "ping" encouraged me to look at the watch on my wrist which alerts me of an incoming message.

I believe the term that the experts use is "tied to technology." When I look at my watch to answer my phone when I should be resting, **inertia** wins and I am resisting success.

I embraced technology to become a better steward of my time, but by using technology and perhaps the lack of discipline, I now have less unoccupied time than ever.

Resisting Success
The Battle Against Inertia

Well, I finally got to sleep, but woke up with a crook in my neck. I can only assume that it was a result of the multiple attempts to look at my watch! Ok I am being a little facetious, but I hope you get my point.

Recently I came to my senses. I choose not to carry my phone nor wear my watch that acts like a phone on Tuesdays. One day each week I choose not to be tied to technology. I remove the watch that acts like phone when I'm resting. I am territorial about my mornings so I don't embrace technology until after 10:00 AM.

Lesson Learned:

The watch that acts like a phone is a wonderful servant, but a horrible master.

Resisting Success

The Battle Against Inertia

Chapter Seven Exercise

List five ways to untie technology

1. _____

2. _____

3. _____

4. _____

5. _____

Chapter Eight

Transfer of Power

Resisting Success
The Battle Against Inertia

I have been a strength coach for over 25 years and have developed a system that allows athletes to transfer the power developed in the weight room to the competition surface. It is common knowledge among strength professionals that the force created by lifting a weight is not equal to the force applied to the track. To be successful it requires a transfer of power. The same principle applies as it relates to knowledge. Knowledge may be defined as the gathering of information or facts. Knowledge carries little value if you fail to apply what you have learned. The name given to the application of knowledge is wisdom and this is when the transfer of power takes place.

I read an interesting article in USA Today that suggested hunching over a mobile device can reduce lung capacity by up to thirty percent. According to Ford's 2016 Trend report *Information Mobile Intelligence*, on average Americans are using their phones 4.7 hours per day. This is disturbing. Another article indicated that

Resisting Success
The Battle Against Inertia

for every inch of forward head posture it can increase the weight of the head on the spine by an additional ten pounds.

For example, in proper postural alignment there is twelve pounds of pressure on the spine. Moving the head foreword two inches doubles the pressure on the spine to twenty-four pounds. If you add an additional inch to this foreword lean the weight on the spine increases to forty-two pounds. Yikes! This makes my back hurt just thinking about it. The article indicated that abnormal leverage from forward drawn heads can (1) Pull the entire spinal column out of alignment, (2) Decrease vital lung capacity by up to thirty percent due to the loss of the cervical lordosis, (3) Decrease inhalation by blocking the action of the hyoid muscles (which help lift the rib when breathing), and (4) Neurologically inhibit peristatic action of the gastrointestinal tract resulting in sluggish bowel syndrome.

Armed with this information I had two choices. Let **inertia** win and do nothing or apply my new-found knowledge, pay attention to my posture when I am on the phone or at the computer and develop my core strength. On this day, I choose wisdom over inertia.

Lesson Learned:

There is a vast difference between knowledge and wisdom. Knowledge is information and facts. Wisdom is the next actionable step which requires us to apply what we have learned. Never leave the moment of inspiration without taking action. Don't let the moment of inspiration get away from you!

Resisting Success
The Battle Against Inertia

Chapter Eight Exercise

The likelihood of doing something diminishes the further away you get from the initial moment of inspiration and your confidence erodes as well.

Identify the moment and topic of inspiration.

_____

_____

The differentiator between an idea that "takes flight" versus one that does not is immediate action.

What is the immediate action you will take?

_____

_____

Action takes on many different forms.

What additional action will you take to maintain your momentum.

_____

_____

Resisting Success

The Battle Against Inertia

Chapter Nine

Making Sense of Failure

"The difference between average people and achieving people is their perception of and response to failure."
John C. Maxwell

Resisting Success

The Battle Against Inertia

No one wants to fail, yet it is inevitable that it is going to happen. Every past success and failure we experience can be a valuable source of information and wisdom. After a failure, no one wants to be *comforted* with the fact that Thomas Edison had nine hundred and ninety-nine attempts before perfecting the light bulb or the multiple failures and setbacks that Abraham Lincoln had between 1831 and 1859 only to become President of the United States in 1860. Success teaches you what you're capable of doing and gives you confidence. However, your failures can often teach greater lessons, and ignite the fire of passion and perseverance if you allow them to. When we recognize that failure is part of the success formula we neutralize inertia and see our failures as stepping stones.

According to the Forbes Magazine (August 2016 issue), Dwayne Johnson, aka "The Rock", is reportedly the highest paid actor in Hollywood hauling in $64.5 million dollars. The truth be known, Hollywood was not a part of his original plans. Johnson

Resisting Success
The Battle Against Inertia

played football for the University of Miami and had a very specific vision for his future; He was going to be the next Michael Strahan, win a Super Bowl with the New York Giants, have a beautiful wife, big house, etc.

As fate would have it, he shredded his left shoulder on the last practice of two-a-days, which resulted in a subsequent surgery. They filled his spot with future hall of famer Warren Sapp. Johnson had four knee surgeries which stunted his development. He ended his University of Miami career with seventy-eight tackles and four sacks. No team in the NFL deemed him worthy to draft so he signed with the Calgary Stampeders of the Canadian Football League and was cut from the squad two months later.

There are many stories about people who have failed, only to find their true calling and go on to make both a significant impact and income. I never thought I'd be doing what I am doing now. I am living and working the dream every day. I've learned to ignore

Resisting Success

The Battle Against Inertia

inertia and embrace struggle. I've learned to make sense of my failures!

> **Lesson Learned:**
>
> Many of us give up to soon. Failure is a significant part of the success formula.

Resisting Success

The Battle Against Inertia

Chapter Nine Exercise

We are the heroes of our own stories.

Revisit (revisit the challenge)

_____

_____

_____

Redefine (Recognize key people and the defining moments.)

_____

_____

_____

Rewrite (A new way of thinking, your perception is your reality.)

_____

_____

_____

Reclaim (Change your trajectory, it takes strength to soar.)

_____

_____

_____

Resisting Success

The Battle Against Inertia

Chapter Ten

Success Entourage

Resisting Success
The Battle Against Inertia

The church that I attend is called Friendship Assembly of God. I have attended this church for several years. Over time I have developed a sincere appreciation for leadership, specifically, our senior pastor, Brad Williamson, and youth pastor, Samuel Thurman. It is not unusual to find the three of us at the local Starbucks discussing life, faith, and leadership. These two gentlemen are part of my "success entourage." We recognize that iron sharpens iron and it is important to choose your friends wisely. When we are at Starbucks or some other location I'm not worried about a thing. Not only are these two armed with the Holy Spirit and the word of God, they also have a physical prowess that's unbelievable. Both pastors are second-degree blackbelts. They represent both lion and lamb and are also the weapon and the warrior.

2 Samuel 23:8-39 describes the exploits of David's Mighty Men, fierce warriors who were loyal to David. There were approximately thirty of the fighting machines, but for the sake of

Resisting Success
The Battle Against Inertia

this story I will choose two. Pastor Brad fits the profile of Josheb-Basshebeth, who was once engulfed in a battle where he raised his spear against eight hundred men, whom he killed in one encounter.

By all indications Pastor Samuel would be Benaiah, a valiant fighter from Kabzeel. The bible reports that he struck down Moab's two mightiest warriors. He also went down into a pit on a snowy day and killed a lion. He also struck down a huge Egyptian. Although the Egyptian had a spear in his hand, Benaiah went against him with a club. He snatched the spear from the Egyptian's hand and killed him with his own spear.

At the age of 56 many people have come and gone in my life. Over time I have experienced the sting of bad friendships and those I've titled "opportunists." I've had my share of encounters with toxic folks as well. They are the individuals that I have allowed to drain my emotional energy. When I chose to embrace the toxic folks, **inertia** wins.

Resisting Success
The Battle Against Inertia

I am thankful for these experiences because they have allowed me to develop criteria for my friendship selection and my circle of influence.

Lesson Learned:

It has been said that we become the sum total of those we spend the most time with. It is my belief that friends don't put friends in compromising positions. Those individuals who are significant in my life I am able to trust with God's money, my wife and my life!

Resisting Success

The Battle Against Inertia

Chapter Ten Exercise

Success Entourage

List five attributes of your success entourage.

1. _____

2. _____

3. _____

4. _____

5. _____

Resisting Success

The Battle Against Inertia

Chapter Eleven

Being Present

Resisting Success
The Battle Against Inertia

For the last few years, I have been afforded the opportunity to provide resiliency coaching at a local community college with a desired outcome of increasing student engagement and success. After several semesters of "crashing the train" we developed a model that demonstrated success. Statistics indicated that the "coaching sessions" made a marked impact in the lives of the student population. Outcomes were measured both qualitatively (collecting individual interviews, participant comments and observations) and quantitatively (collecting numerical measurable data).

My purpose in life is to create a positive change in the lives of others, to motivate, educate and inspire them to develop greater expectations within themselves. Providing resiliency training to this group of students has been one of the most impactful opportunities I have ever had. It takes approximately thirty-five minutes to drive from my home to the college campus. The front range of Colorado boasts the Rocky Mountains and its panoramic view is

Resisting Success
The Battle Against Inertia

breathtaking. It is so beautiful that it looks like the background of a movie set. Half the time I expect to see John Wayne or Clint Eastwood coming down the mountain on a horse.

The landscape, however, is also colored with unrealized potential. This unrealized potential comes in the form of people, young and old, either by choice, circumstance or both who lack the drive or ability to advance their lives. As a servant coach, it is a difficult thing to see. Stepping into the classroom at the community college is like a breath of fresh air. It is an opportunity to give wings to the student's dreams and bring their education to life.

Last semester I presented 112 times over the course of about ten weeks. Each message lasted forty-five minutes or so. The topics of discussion varied from behavior modification to personal mastery. Each class had a different vibe which guaranteed a unique experience. This was sensational. I had a captive audience and could fulfill my purpose in life. Each day I had a chance to collaborate with a professor and Encourage, Educate

Resisting Success
The Battle Against Inertia

and Equip the audience with tools that I believed would help position them for the best chance of success.

About half way though the semester I started to recognize various behavior patterns and responses to the messaging. In most cases the students were excited to see me, fully engaged, taking notes, and asking questions. While walking through the halls there was no sweeter sound than a student saying, "Hello Coach Lee, how are you doing today?"

Other days students were less enthusiastic. I would leave the classroom bewildered, wondering where the challenge was coming from. Was it the ebb and flow of life or perhaps an arc of distortion in the room resulting in a disconnect?

Effective communication can be difficult, often the message sent is not the message received. Even clearly written or stated words can be misinterpreted and misunderstood, especially when filtered through the sieve of prejudice and preconception.

Resisting Success
The Battle Against Inertia

My friend, John Register, is a professional speaker. He has helped me grow by leaps and bounds both personally and professionally. He says "Charmas there is the message that you prepare, the message you present and the message that the audience hears!" Perhaps my communication was mitigated or not direct enough. I learned about mitigated speech in Malcolm Gladwell's book *Outliers*. Gladwell defines mitigation as "any attempt to downplay or sugarcoat the meaning of what is being said."

There is a delicate balance when I am speaking to a large group. When I communicate more directly for some it may come across as brash, harsh, or too forceful, for others indirect and soft. Perhaps I am the problem.

Nonetheless the behaviors caught my attention and I began to wonder how I was showing up in life. Does the speaker (wife, pastor, coach, etc.) have my full attention? Am I distracted?

Resisting Success
The Battle Against Inertia

How often do I sabotage myself with a negative attitude or some other pattern of behavior that I am not aware of? How many ways am I allowing **inertia** to win by not showing up in the **strength of my highest self**? How many times have I settled for a lesser version of myself and **resisted success**?

Lesson Learned:

When I act from the strength of my highest self, I bring a positive attitude energy and joy to most situations. I have learned to check in with myself and have become more aware of the message I send to others with my body language etc.

Resisting Success
The Battle Against Inertia

Chapter Eleven Exercise

Act from the strength of my highest self. This is a conscious choice to show up as your best self in every situation.

The way I would describe my highest self is;

1._____

2._____

3._____

I know when I am acting from my best self when;

1._____

2._____

3._____

I can consciously remind myself to be at my best self by;

1._____

2._____

3._____

Resisting Success

The Battle Against Inertia

Chapter Twelve

Keep Your Eyes on The Shoreline

Resisting Success
The Battle Against Inertia

There was a young lady named Florence Chadwick who today would be the equivalent of Michael Phelps. She was the first woman to swim the English Channel in both directions. Chadwick was very ambitious. After some serious thought, she decided to do what many believed was impossible, at least for a woman. She wanted to be the first woman to swim twenty-one miles from the Catalina Islands to the California shore. A handful of men had performed the feat and had success, however not all were successful. With a launch date of July 4, 1952 Chadwick prepared for the challenge. She realized that her preparation would breed a tremendous amount of confidence. Finally, the day came and on this 4th of July morning she was greeted by a thick dense fog and cool temperatures. The water was bone chilling cold. Nonetheless she dove into the water and began the journey. Millions of people were watching on national television with great anticipation.

On both sides of Chadwick were boats occupied with men who carried rifles and sticks. Several times, sharks which had gotten too close had to be driven away with rifles to protect her in the water. Fearless and confident Chadwick swam for fifteen hours but the cold water and dense fog began to take their toll. The fatigue became insurmountable and Chadwick motioned to the people in the boats that she was finished. They told her that she was near the shore, urging her not to quit but all she could see was the dense fog.

With **victory out of sight**, Chadwick conceded to the cold and the fog. She had been pulled out only a half mile from the California shore. A few hours later there was a news interview. Chadwick indicated that she was not defeated by her fatigue or the cold. She believed that she could have made it, if she only could have seen the shore. Two months later she swam the same channel, and again fog obscured her view, but this time she swam with her faith intact – somewhere behind that fog was land. Not only was she the first woman to swim the Catalina Island to the California shore, but she beat the men's record by some two hours!

Resisting Success

The Battle Against Inertia

Lesson Learned:

With victory out of sight, Chadwick conceded to the cold and the fog. She believed that she would have made it, if she could have only seen the shore line. The fog and the cold were distractions. It is important to keep a front side focus. When an individual begins to experience obstacles, road blocks, physical or emotional pain in the heat of battle, the brain whose primary role is self-preservation asks the question, "Why must I suffer?" **CHAMPIONS** will answer the question with the vision they have carefully constructed and will continue to fight. Most, however, do not possess a **vision,** and quit when they hit a bump in the road or when the pain kicks in.

Resisting Success
The Battle Against Inertia

Chapter Twelve Exercise

What would your life look like victorious in the following areas if you keep your eyes on the shoreline and don't get derailed by the fog?

Personal:

_____

_____

_____

Family:

_____

_____

_____

Community:

_____

_____

_____

Professional:

_____

_____

_____

Resisting Success

The Battle Against Inertia

Chapter Thirteen

Forgiveness

Resisting Success
The Battle Against Inertia

I have lived long enough to have stumbled a few times. In other word's I have made my share of mistakes. On the other hand, I have experienced heartbreak, been misled, mistreated and betrayed. In these types of situations, it is easy to become upset, harbor hatred, anger and resentment.

I have learned the hard way that resentment and anger cannot co-exist. They are incompatible with peace and joy. I have carried the emotional baggage and experienced the physiological repercussions that go hand-in-hand with these feelings and they can result in a very unhealthy state of being.

Some of you reading this book may have had similar experiences and continue to carry the emotional scars and physiological aches and pains. Well I have good news for you, there is an answer. It is called forgiveness. When we chose not to forgive, it is the equivalent of drinking poison. We become toxic and contaminate not only ourselves but those around us. As long as we embrace **inertia** instead of forgiveness, we become a lesser version of ourselves and stay locked in an emotional prison. First and foremost, forgive yourself for the wreckage you may have created in your own life. Secondly, forgive those who may have created wreckage in your life. When you do so you free yourself from the bitterness and pain. By the way, when you forgive them it's not about them it's about you. Thirdly, if there is someone whom you may have wronged, ask them for forgiveness. It is up to them to accept or decline your request. Embrace the freedom that comes with forgiveness.

Resisting Success

The Battle Against Inertia

Lesson Learned:

To err is human to forgive is divine. There is power in forgiveness. This reminds me of the song *Already Gone* which was performed in 1974, by an American rock and roll band called The Eagles. There is a line in the song that says, "*So often times it happens, that we live our lives in chains, and we never even know we have the key.* We hold the key to forgiveness! If it's meant to be its up to me.

Resisting Success

The Battle Against Inertia

Chapter Thirteen Exercise

Forgiveness

Name three things that you can forgive yourself for.

1._____

2._____

3._____

Name three people to forgive.

1._____

2._____

3._____

Name three people that you'd like to forgive you.

1._____

2._____

3._____

Resisting Success
The Battle Against Inertia

References

Maxwell, John C. (2000) Failing Forward; Turning Mistakes into Stepping Stones for Success; Thomas Nelson Publishers

Shipnuck, A. (December 5, 2016) Dwayne Johnson Owns Hollywood. Sports Illustrated, 28-34

Burchard, Brendon (2014) The Motivation Manifesto, 9 Declarations to Claim Your Personal Power, Hay House Inc.

Swindoll, Charles (2005) So You Want To Be Like Christ? Eight Essentials To Get You There. W. Publishing Group, a division of Thomas Nelson Inc.

McGraw, C. Phillip (1999) Life Strategies, Doing What Works, Doing What Matters, Hyperion New York

Loehr, J., & Schwartz, T. (2003) *The Power of Full Engagement, Managing Energy, Not Time, Is the Key to High Performance and Personal Renewal.* New York: The Free Press

Covey, S. (1989) *The Seven Habits of Highly Effective People, Powerful Lessons in Personal Change.* New York: Free Press

Simpson, Joanne C. Digital disabilities — text neck, cellphone elbow — are painful and growing
https://www.washingtonpost.com/national/health-science/digital-disabilities--text-neck-cellphone-elbow--are-painful-and-growing/2016/06/13/df070c7c-0afd-11e6-a6b6-2e6de3695b0e_story.html?utm_term=.cd6dd4f8fc75

Resisting Success
The Battle Against Inertia

Dalton, E. Text Neck and Desktop Neck EriIDalton.com (February 21, 2017) 7-1-2017

   http://erikdalton.com/blog/text-neck-desktop-neck/

Mehmet Kandemir and Mehmet Palanc. Academic Functional Procrastination: Validity and Reliability Study, Procedia-Social and Behavioral Sciences (October 7, 2014) 8-1-2017

   http://www.sciencedirect.com/science/article/pii/S1877042814052471

Conan, Neil. How to Be a Productive Procrastinator, npr.org/diversions, npr, (June 12, 2008) 7-27-2017

   http://www.npr.org/templates/story/story.php?storyId=91432804

Made in the USA
San Bernardino, CA
09 February 2020